HAVE FUN READING THIS BOOK!

IT OFFERS SOME REAL SURVIVAL TIPS. BUT THE SETTINGS ARE NOT REAL. THINK ABOUT HOW YOU CAN USE THESE HACKS IN REAL LIFE. USE COMMON SENSE. BE SAFE AND ASK AN ADULT FOR PERMISSION AND HELP WHEN NEEDED.

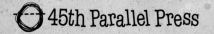
45th Parallel Press

Published in the United States of America by Cherry Lake Publishing
Ann Arbor, Michigan
www.cherrylakepublishing.com

Reading Adviser: Marla Conn, MS, Ed., Literacy specialist, Read-Ability, Inc.
Book Designer: Felicia Macheske

Photo Credits: © Jurik Peter/Shutterstock.com, cover; © Ink Drop/Shutterstock.com, 5; © Beril Yamac/
Shutterstock.com, 5; © Leah-Anne Thompson/Shutterstock.com, 6; © runzelkorn/Shutterstock.com, 9;
© Elisanth/Shutterstock.com, 11; © Hein Nouwens/Shutterstock.com, 12; © tarapong srichaiyos/Shutterstock.
com, 13; © pathdoc/Shutterstock.com, 14; © Oxie99/Shutterstock.com, 17; © bjphotographs/Shutterstock.
com, 19; © Lightkite/Shutterstock.com, 20; © Georgy Markov/Shutterstock.com, 21; © Anna Cinaroglu/
Shutterstock.com, 22; © rnl/Shutterstock.com, 25; © Viktor1/Shutterstock.com, 27; © aperturesound/
Shutterstock.com, 29

Other Images Throughout: © SrsPvl Witch/Shutterstock.com; © Igor Vitkovskiy/Shutterstock.com; © FabrikaSimf/
Shutterstock.com; © bulbspark/Shutterstock.com; © donatas1205/Shutterstock.com; © NinaM/Shutterstock.
com; © Picsfive/Shutterstock.com; © prapann/Shutterstock.com; © S_Kuzmin/Shutterstock.com © autsawin
uttisin/Shutterstock.com; © xpixel/Shutterstock.com; © OoddySmile/Shutterstock.com; © ilikestudio/
Shutterstock.com; © Kues/Shutterstock.com; © ankomando/Shutterstock.com ; © Hein Nouwens/Shutterstock.
com; © SunshineVector/Shutterstock.com; © Lightkite/Shutterstock.com; © Bakai/Shutterstock.com; © Rauf
Aliyev/Shutterstock.com

45th Parallel Press is an imprint of Cherry Lake Publishing.

Library of Congress Cataloging-in-Publication Data

Names: Loh-Hagan, Virginia, author.
Title: Witching hour hacks / by Virginia Loh-Hagan.
Description: Ann Arbor, MI : Cherry Lake Publishing, [2019] | Series: Could
 you survive? | Includes bibliographical
 references and index.
Identifiers: LCCN 2019006168| ISBN 9781534147843 (hardcover) | ISBN
 9781534150706 (pbk.) | ISBN 9781534149274 (pdf) | ISBN 9781534152137
 (hosted ebook)
Subjects: LCSH: Survival—Juvenile literature. | Supernatural—Juvenile literature.
Classification: LCC GF86 .L64275 2019 | DDC 613.6/9—dc23
LC record available at https://lccn.loc.gov/2019006168

Cherry Lake Publishing would like to acknowledge the work of The Partnership for 21st Century Skills.
Please visit *www.p21.org* for more information.

Printed in the United States of America
Corporate Graphics

Dr. Virginia Loh-Hagan is an author, university professor, former classroom teacher, and curriculum
designer. She wrote the 45th Parallel Press series called Magic, Myth, and Mystery. This series is about
supernatural creatures. Loh-Hagan lives in San Diego with her very tall husband and very naughty dogs.
To learn more about her, visit www.virginialoh.com.

INTRODUCTION 4

CHAPTER 1
STAY ALERT! 11

CHAPTER 2
KEEP THE LIGHT ON! 15

CHAPTER 3
FEEL THE HEAT! 19

CHAPTER 4
PLAY A PRANK! 23

CHAPTER 5
HIT YOUR MARK! 27

DID YOU KNOW? 30

CONSIDER THIS! 31

LEARN MORE 31

GLOSSARY 32

INDEX 32

COULD YOU SURVIVE
WITCHING HOUR?

THIS BOOK COULD SAVE YOUR LIFE!

The **witching hour** is a time of night. Some people think it's an hour after midnight. Some people think it's between midnight and dawn. Some people think it's between 3:00 a.m. and 4:00 a.m.

The witching hour is dangerous. It's also known as the "devil's hour." It's when **supernatural** beings come out. Supernatural means belonging to some magical energy. These beings are the strongest at this time. They have great powers. Supernatural things are beyond science. They're beyond the rules of nature. They're beyond the knowledge of man.

○
○
TIP Wear good luck charms.

During the witching hour, beware of strange things. Beware of witches. Beware of ghosts. Beware of vampires. Especially beware of **demons**. Demons love the witching hour. They're evil. They cause harm. They kill. They're hunters. They hunt humans. They eat humans' bodies. They eat humans' souls.

There are more humans than demons. Humans are able to control demons during the day. But they're less safe at night. Most demons are **nocturnal**. Nocturnal means active at night. The wall between the living and dead weakens during the witching hour. Humans are at risk during this time.

TIP Think positive thoughts.

But you might be one of the lucky survivors. You have to be smart. First, learn all you can about supernatural beings. Second, find ghost hunters. These are people who know about the supernatural.

Most importantly, know how to survive. Keep this in mind:

- You can only live 3 minutes without air.

- You can only live 3 days without water.

- You can only live 3 weeks without food.

This book offers you survival **hacks**, or tricks. Always be prepared. Good luck to you.

TIP Go to the library. Learn about ways to fight demons.

9

SCIENCE CONNECTION

The witching hour could be related to sleep disorders. Disorders are sicknesses. Some people have sleeping problems. They're tired. They can't fully sleep. They can't be fully awake. They may hallucinate. This means they see things that aren't there. Their minds play tricks on them. Sleep hallucinations feel real. Dreams happen when people are completely asleep. Hallucinations happen when people are somewhat awake. They happen when people are falling asleep or waking up. People can see things. They can hear voices. They can feel things. Waking up at 3:00 a.m. is not normal. This may confuse people. This may make people think they see demons. People with anxiety or depression may have trouble sleeping. Stress can also cause hallucinations. About 40 percent of adults have sleep hallucinations. Children don't really have them. There are other sleep disorders. An example is sleepwalking. This is when people walk while asleep. Some people may have nightmares. Nightmares are bad dreams.

CHAPTER 1

STAY ALERT!

Oh no! It's 3:00 a.m. You're sleepy. Make a noisy sound trap. Hear when demons are coming. Use shakers to make music. This will help you stay awake.

TIP Hang wind chimes. Demons hate them. Wind chimes also move when there's movement.

HACK

1. Gather tin cans with lids, like a can for breath mints.

2. Gather things that'll make noise. Examples are beans, coins, and paper clips.

3. Make several holes in the lids. Use a hammer and nail.

4. Put things inside the cans. Shake to make noise.

5. Wrap a rubber band around each can.

6. Get several long ropes. Tie several cans to them. Put ropes on the floor in different places. Demons may trip over them. You'll hear them coming.

7. Put cans in drawers. Demons may open them. You can hear the cans roll.

TIP Play music. Sing along. Stay awake.

explained by

STEM

The key to this hack is the holes.

Holes **amplify** sounds. Amplify means to make louder. Holes change how air flows.

Sound is **vibrations**. Vibrations are waves. They move up and down. When an object vibrates, air **particles** move. Particles are tiny bits. They bump into other particles. They vibrate the air inside your ear. That's when you hear sounds.

Amplitude is the height of the sound wave. Changing the amplitude changes its loudness. Sound waves vibrate inside and around the opening of holes. They travel around the rest of the area. Everything vibrates more freely. Holes let sound waves inside the can travel outside the can.

CHAPTER 2

KEEP THE LIGHT ON!

Lights will keep you awake. They'll also let you see in the dark. Make your own **lantern**. Lanterns are covered lights. They can be moved.

HACK

1. Get an empty soda can. Put on a pair of protective gloves.

2. Cut a slit. Start 1 inch (2.5 centimeters) from the top of the can. Cut horizontally until you are about halfway around the can.

3. Do the same at the bottom of the can.

4. Cut a slit in the center of your 2 cuts. Go down the can. This will create 2 flaps. Open the flaps. This should look like an open door.

5. Bend the soda tab so it's sticking up.

6. Attach wire or string to the tab. This can be your handle.

7. Put a candle inside the can.

TIP Get a dog. Dogs bark at intruders.

STEM

The key to this hack is **reflection**.

Reflection is the throwing back of light without absorbing it. Light travels in rays. It travels in straight lines. It does this until it hits something. In this hack, light hits the flaps. The flaps reflect the light back. They reflect light from the candle's flame.

The soda can is made of **aluminum**. Aluminum is a metal. The flaps are flat. They act like a mirror. Light reflects at the same angle as it hit the flaps. If the aluminum were crinkled, this hack wouldn't work as well. The angles in the surface would reflect light in different directions.

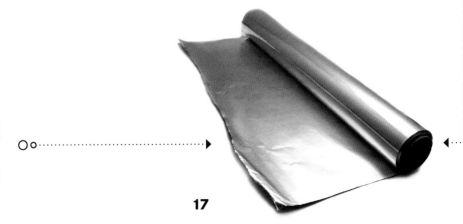

REAL-LIFE CONNECTION

Today, some people practice Wicca. Wicca is a religion that believes in magic. It practices witchcraft. It worships nature. It doesn't worship demons. Its code is "If it harm none, do what you will." It has covens. Covens are groups of witches. Each coven has about 10 to 15 witches. By the 1980s, there were about 50,000 Wiccans in Europe and North America. The major festivals of Wicca are called sabbats. There are 8 main sabbats. They mark changes in the seasons. They begin at sunset. They end at sunset the next day. They hold rites at night. They light candles or make bonfires. Rites are special acts. They're traditions. A popular rite involves a black cloth. The cloth is held above people's heads. It's cut with a knife in the center. This opens the 2 worlds. At the end, the black cloth is sewn back up.

CHAPTER 3

FEEL THE HEAT!

Some people have seen ghosts and demons. They say they felt chilly. They felt cold spots. Stay warm. Make a heater.

TIP Burn sage. Sage is used to clean a house of bad spirits.

HACK

1. Get small candles. Put in a metal pan. Put them close together. Light them.

2. Put a grill rack on top of pan.

3. Use gloves when handling. Materials can get really hot.

4. Get a small **terra-cotta** flowerpot. Terra-cotta is a type of building material. It's made of earth.

5. Put a small pot upside down on the grill rack. The open side should be over the candles.

6. Cover the pot holes with foil.

7. Get a larger flowerpot. Put over the smaller one. Put upside down.

TIP Pay attention to strange sounds and smells.

STEM

The key to this hack is **convection**.

Convection is when heat moves in and out of an object. It's caused by the movement of surrounding air or water.

The candles act like a **burner**. Burners make heat. The small pot works as the convector. It gets heat from the candles. The foil traps the heat in the smaller pot. It helps cause the convection. Without the foil, most of the heat would escape. The heat would escape through the holes in the pot. The large pot acts like a **radiator**. Radiators transfer heat to the outside. The air between the pots is heated. It comes out through the gaps.

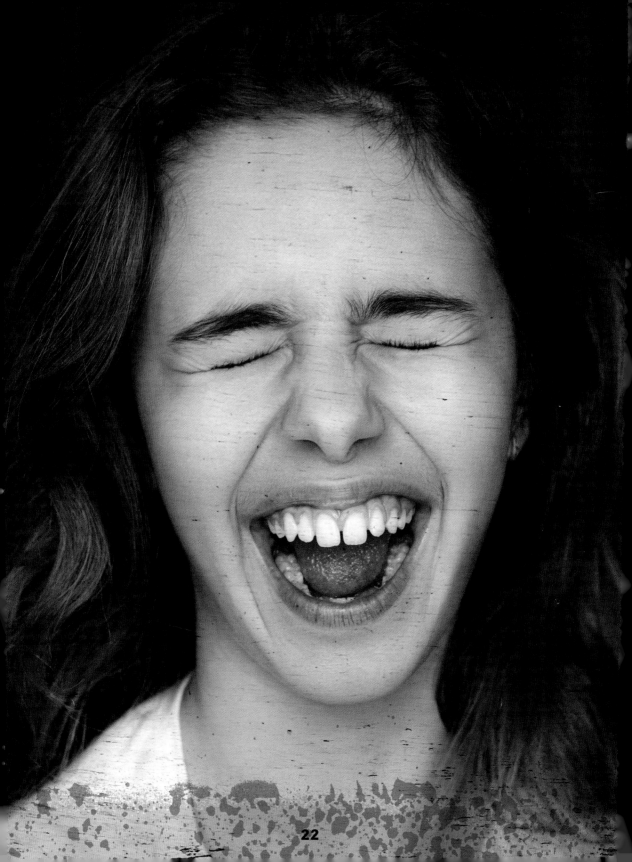

CHAPTER 4

PLAY A PRANK!

You won't be able to beat demons. Demons are stronger. They're magical. So, trick them. Plan a **prank**. Pranks are jokes. This will give you time to run away!

TIP Laugh very loudly. Be happy. Demons feed on sadness.

HACK

1. Thread a needle with string.

2. Stick the needle in the middle of a Mentos mint. Thread it through. Tie a strong knot.

3. Remove the needle from the string. Leave some extra thread. Knot the end.

4. Get a large Diet Coke bottle.

5. Lower the Mentos into the bottle. Let the Mentos dangle.

6. Leave the extra string outside of the bottle.

7. Screw on the lid. The lid should hold the string in place.

8. Cut off the extra string.

9. Leave all around the house. Wait for the demons to get thirsty. Offer a soda!

STEM

The key to this hack is the Mentos.

Mentos are a mint candy. Its surface has thousands of small **pores**. Pores are tiny holes. Mentos create bubble growth sites. They let gas bubbles form quickly. The bubbles form on the Mentos' surface.

The bubbles grow. They float. They burst out of the soda. They keep forming. This makes a nice, foamy **geyser**. Geysers are jets of water.

The **ingredients** of the Mentos and Diet Coke help. Ingredients are the things that make up a dish. The sugar and other things help bubbles form faster. They lower the surface layer of the **liquid**.

TIP Be polite. Ask demons to leave.

SPOTLIGHT BIOGRAPHY

Mercy Lena Brown lived in Rhode Island. She died in 1891. She died of a lung sickness. Some of her family members also died of it. People thought the Brown family was haunted. They thought they were vampires. Brown was buried. Her dead body was removed from its tomb. Brown's dead body didn't have any signs of rot. It still had blood in her heart. So, she was called a vampire. In truth, her tomb was above ground. The weather was cold. Her body didn't rot because it was frozen. But people didn't understand this. They blamed the supernatural. They burned her heart and liver. They buried what was left of her. No grass grows on her grave. People think this is proof she's a vampire. Others think people just stomp out the grass. Some people say they feel a chill. They see Brown's ghost walking around.

CHAPTER 5

HIT YOUR MARK!

You might need to defend yourself. Be ready. Make a **slingshot**. Slingshots are tools. They're used to hit small things. Only shoot to protect yourself.

TIP Make a circle of salt. Do this around yourself.

HACK

1. Get a plastic bottle with a large lid. Take off the cap.

2. Cut off the bottom of the bottle.

3. Get a balloon. Cut off the **narrow** part. Narrow means thin.

4. Stretch the balloon over the opening.

5. Use rubber bands and tape to secure the ballon. Make sure the balloon is tightly wrapped around the opening.

6. Put items inside the balloon. (Dip items in **holy** water. Holy means godly. Demons hate holy water.)

7. Stretch out the balloon. Aim and shoot.

TIP Save your energy. Use it to fight demons.

STEM

The key to this hack is the **transformation** of energy.

Transformation means a change. The energy from pulling back is not lost. It just changes into another form.

Work is a combination of **force** and **distance**. Force is how hard the balloon is pulled. Distance is how far back the balloon is pulled. Pulling the balloon creates work. This work is stored as **elastic energy**. Elastic energy is energy stored in a stretchy object. It's used to shoot things at high speeds.

When the balloon is released, elastic energy changes into **kinetic energy**. Kinetic energy is moving energy. The flying item is kinetic energy. When it hits something and stops, kinetic energy becomes heat.

DID YOU KNOW?

- The most dangerous night of all is Halloween. Halloween is October 31. It started with the ancient Celts. Ancient Celts lived 2,000 years ago. They lived around Ireland. They celebrated their new year on November 1. So, October 31 was the last day of the year. It was the start of winter. It was when the dead came back to earth. Celts left out food. They made fires. They wore costumes. They wanted to protect themselves from evil spirits.

- Throughout history, people were scared of witches. They accused people of being witches. They'd kill them. A common way was to burn them at the stake. Stakes are pointed posts in the ground. Some women went outside during the witching hour. They were called witches.

- Psychologists study the human mind. Some psychologists link the witching hour to melatonin. Melatonin is a hormone. It's in our bodies. It regulates our sleeping and waking schedule. It's at its peak between 11:00 p.m. and 3:00 a.m. Some psychologists think humans are most confused during this time. They sense or see things that aren't there.

- In the late afternoon, babies and young children turn into monsters. They get cranky. They're fussy. They cry. They act up. They need naps. Mothers call this the "witching hour." Luckily, children grow out of this.

- The occult is a belief in the supernatural. In the occult, the number 3 is creepy. Demons knock 3 times. They say your name 3 times. They howl 3 times. Anything that comes in threes is bad.

CONSIDER THIS!

TAKE A POSITION!

Think about what could be haunting the witching hour. Make a list of creatures from movies that you've seen. Which are the scariest? Why do you think so? Argue your point with reasons and evidence.

SAY WHAT?

Demonology is the study of demons. Pick a demon. Read more about the demon. Describe the demon. Explain the demon's powers. Explain the demon's weaknesses.

THINK ABOUT IT!

There are things people can't explain. When this happens, they blame the supernatural. They make up stories to explain things. Have you ever made up stories? Have you ever lied? What did you say and why? What were you covering up?

LEARN MORE!

Lewis, J. Patrick, and Gerald Kelley (illust.). *M Is for Monster: A Fantastic Creatures Alphabet*. Ann Arbor, MI: Sleeping Bear Press, 2014.

Loh-Hagan, Virginia. *Ghost Hunter*. Ann Arbor, MI: Cherry Lake Publishing, 2015.

Sautter, Aaron. *A Field Guide to Goblins, Gremlins, and Other Wicked Creatures*. Mankato, MN: Capstone Press, 2015.

GLOSSARY

aluminum (uh-LOO-mih-nuhm) metal

amplify (AM-plih-fye) to make sounds louder

amplitude (AM-plih-tood) the height of sound waves

burner (BUR-nur) a tool that makes heat

convection (kuhn-VEK-shuhn) the process of heat moving in and out of an object

demons (DEE-muhnz) monsters and other supernatural beings

distance (DIS-tuhns) the amount of space between two things or people

elastic energy (ih-LAS-tik EN-ur-jee) energy stored in an object like something stretchy or coily

force (FORS) strength, push or pull

geyser (GYE-zur) a strong jet of water

hacks (HAKS) tricks

holy (HOH-lee) godly

ingredients (in-GREE-dee-uhnts) things that are combined to make up a dish or substance

kinetic energy (kih-NET-ik EN-ur-jee) moving energy

lantern (LAN-turn) a covered light that can be moved

liquid (LIK-wid) water form

narrow (NAR-oh) thin

nocturnal (nahk-TUR-nuhl) active at night

particles (PAHR-tih-kuhlz) tiny bits of matter

pores (PORZ) tiny holes

prank (PRANGK) a joke

radiator (RAY-dee-ay-tur) a tool that transfers heat to the outside

reflection (rih-FLEKT-shuhn) the throwing back of light, heat, or sound without being absorbed

slingshot (SLING-shaht) a tool used to hit small things

supernatural (soo-pur-NACH-ur-uhl) belonging to a magical force that is beyond the knowledge of science and man

terra-cotta (ter-uh-KAH-tuh) earthenware building material

transformation (trans-for-MAY-shuhn) change

vibrations (vye-BRAY-shuhnz) rapid back-and-forth movement of waves

witching hour (WICH-ing OUR) a time of night in which the veil between the living and dead is thin

INDEX

aluminum, 17
amplification, 13
amplitude, 13

bubbles, 25

convection, 21

distance, 29

elastic energy, 29
energy transformation, 29

force, 29

heater, 19–21
holes, 13

kinetic energy, 29

lantern, 15–17
light rays, 17
Mentos, 24, 25
music, 11–13

particles, 13
pores, 25
prank, 23–25

radiator, 21
reflection, **17**

sleep disorders, 10
slingshot, 27–29
sound waves, 13
supernatural beings, 4, 8
survival, 8

vampire, 26
vibrations, 13

Wicca, 18
witching hour, 4–10, 30